KIRBY

Dedication page

Made with Love by Teresa Hounslow

So I decided to save money on trips away with my Family as Hotels cost so much.

This is my journey from start to not quite finished.

VW T25

Dedicated to my children

C.S.J.P.S

This is where my journey begins, wish me luck. This is how Kirby came to me, lovely in it's day but now dated and in need of a make over. I think this may be my calling as I've been itching to get my hands on a projects for years.   I've always wanted a VW camper wasn't sure what model I wanted but I'm very happy with this one and highly recommend them. If you think you want one, when you finally do, you wont regret it.

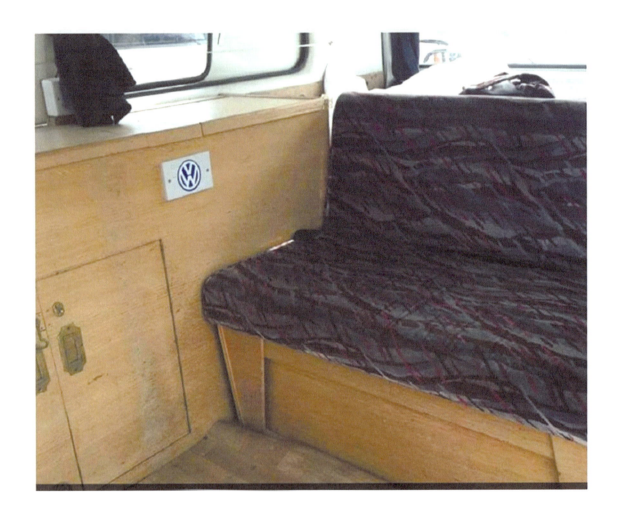

The curtains were quite sun bleached and the woodwork had soaked in too much moisture. I attempted to sew a lining onto these original curtains and although it made a great black out, it still wasn't good enough even up to my standards. Here I'm still at the deciding part of my journey what colours do I go for, and most of all where on earth do I start ? It was a long road ahead.

Here I decided to cover the roof windows in self adhesive felt material, because I didn't want to be woken too early by the sunrise. This was sold as scrap cuts offs and very cheap, again keeping in with the low budget. It's also removable if ever I change my mind and very easy to attach. I used a Stanley knife to cut the surplus away.

Well this was just for a bit of fun adding the bunting to the top side windows, it also helps block a little more light as that's my preference, each to their own. Here you can see the top right shelf in its original colour, and below the shelf the carpet has seen its last days, time for a change. At this point I'm racing with ideas but it is a long process of elimination to get to where I'd like it to be.

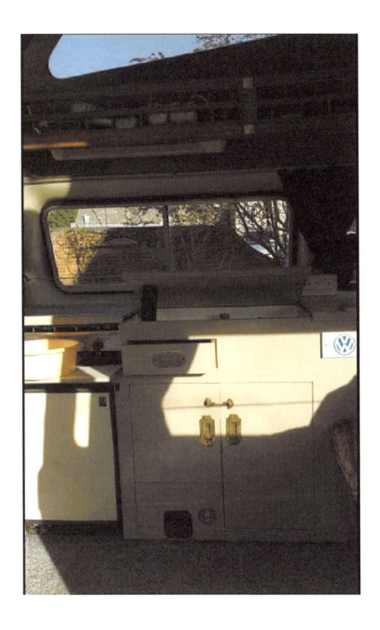

This is my first layer of undercoat onto the wood unit in hope to give it a fresh look. Here you can see the original carpet and shelf too. I'm not perfect at painting I make many mistakes, but again it's about having a go.   I used a simple wood primer, as they say the secret is in the preparation.   Also I would suggest sanding the area well prior to painting. Remember it's all about customising it to your needs and at the end of the day it's only you who needs to love it, you may take criticism but don't let anybody else's personal taste deter you from your project, you can change anything further down the line.

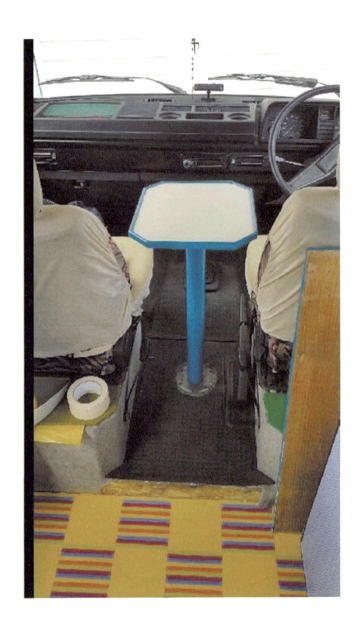

So here I have sprayed the table underneath, down the leg and also round the sides. Just to save money on replacing them as they were very worn. In the light of day I originally wanted all pastel colours but I couldn't find what I wanted, and once I get it in my mind to do something I take what I can afford at the time. This way has always been beneficial in the past to stick with as low budget as possible. There is all sorts of things you could do here for example: felt material around the leg for texture or mask it up adding stripes or squares, anything to add your own touches.

Sitting here in the dark contemplating what to do next. I have given the shelf above a coat of gloss white paint thinking it would brighten it up, but here is a common mistake I have learned is shiny paint shows every little imperfection. I'm also considering cutting the shelf down one level as well to make it easier to grab items. Sometimes I think why am I doing this am I making it worse, yes I have as many doubts as the next person. But I will say this never give up keep going.

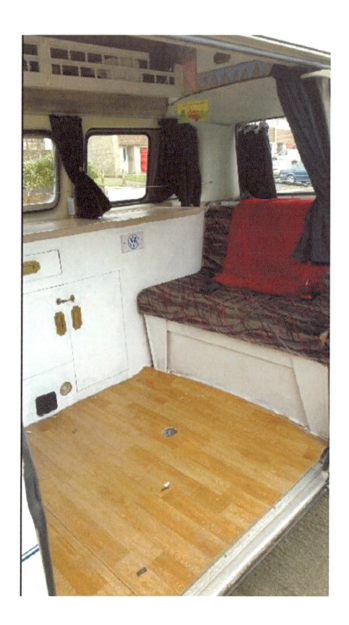

Again I have used gloss only due to the fact I had some in my garage and it kept me within my very low budget this way. There is lino here over the carpet I suppose it was there to protect it, but I thought I'm going to change the lot, after all I'd managed to find a roll of carpet from a charity shop for only £1.00 I couldn't resist it as it was brand new the perfect size and rubber backed. Not the colour I would of chosen but a very satisfying thing to save money wouldn't you agree? So the flooring was taken out.

Maybe I got carried away with the felt, well it's different that's for sure. This kind of thing is very easy, all you need is a Stanley knife or a pair of scissors to cut the self adhesive material. I believe you can get all kinds of textures, how about a faux leather. A tip...do not go too bright here in the dash area as you will get reflections in the glass, you can't afford any distractions to avert your safety. But remember you can also paint this area but the paint that sticks to dash boards was not in my budget. I used what I already had at home in our arts and crafts box, or you could just glue your material down.

The gloss on this shelf didn't look great as I'm not very good at painting with a brush I don't mind admitting, It's fine I will laugh about it later, but I certainly do not want to do all those little posts twice. As you can see under the shelf I used the felt material again, I know myself too well this will not stay this way very long. It did stick very well to the carpet that was already there. Apparently there is material sprays to if you're looking for a cheap option to colour your van ceilings. Don't let your budget stop you doing something think of all the material you have in your airing cupboard.

The worktop had soaked in a lot of moisture so I decided to take it out including the lid to the sink. Most of the unit was ok, I'm guessing the window may have been left open in the past, and only the top surface was damaged. Shall we move on......

I made a mistake here by using the wrong wood, but I had it in my garage and it was free, so down the line I shall change it when it needs it. But I advise you to use marine ply as its better where there is moisture in the air. Another great idea is to buy kitty litter and pour it into socks , tie the ends up and place them round the van, it will soak up the condensation, especially in winter if you store it during that time.

The carpet here on the ceiling isn't in the best shape but determined to carry on and oh look I used felt. At this stage I really thought I was doing well and getting somewhere but later down the line I know I will be thinking I can do better as this is hiding the problem.   What I really need to do is rip out the old carpet with marks on it. That's my advice take it out, do not settle for any dirty looking things just get rid of them, if they are cosmetic.

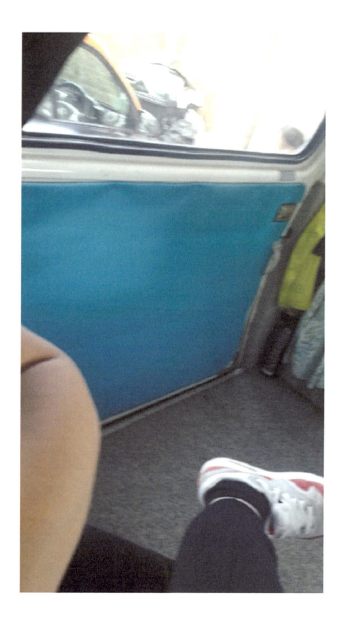

I have used some faux leather material I had left over to cover the door card. I used glue on the reverse to keep it in place and then the screws that hold the door card on secure it as well. This is where it all starts to take shape and colour adds some brightness. All I need now is some nice weather as at this time of year it seems to be non stop rain. We want to go away and test it out. Back to the subject, you will need to pop off the panels to recover. I would suggest a strong glue to fix the material over the back, as staples will go through the board.

Nope not good enough, let's see what I can rip out next. I have given the unit a coat of white paint which I had already in my garage again a budget thing. I covered the fridge here in a sticky back material called Fablon, but later discovered it doesn't work, as in my taste, so that had to be taken out. This isn't over yet KIRBY.

So I pull off the wheel trims and buying new wheels is out of the question, so what can I do.....PAINT!   I think the wheels are quite nice I've seen worse. Doing this while they are still on the van isn't going to give the best results obviously not as good as sending them to be dipped. But the point is budget, and things like taking off wheels I leave to a mechanic. Just mask up the wheels well and choose a nice dry sunny day, paint with a brush or spray from a can, if you go wrong wait a few days sand it down and try again as you need to build up a good layer of paint anyway.

Let's pose, so we decided to take Kirby for a little spin to the beach, the weather was perfect. We had a lot of onlookers trying to see into the van at this stage and we spent the night because we were enjoying ourselves so much. The joys of it being free for us to sleep over made it even more delightful.

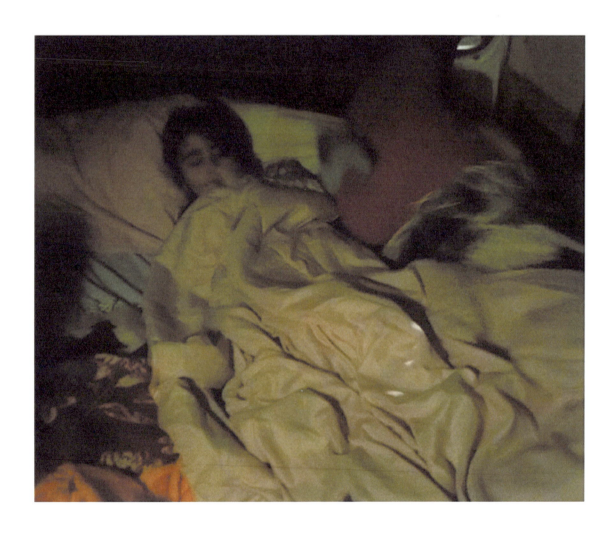

After a hard day playing in the sand.

The joys of camping and getting to wake up to a view of the sea for free. So I shall sit here for a while drinking my coffee and maybe do some more changes as I took a lot of my arts and crafts items along with me just in case I felt inspiration.

Ok bring the beach inside, and why not. Just think of all the things we could make from these to decorate Kirby with, I think a seaside theme would be quite beautiful.

If you go camping these are great, although I have two main heaters in the van I have this back up heater in case I run out of gas in the large bottle. Warm Fuzzy Cosy!

Finally I get to paint the wheels, I wasn't expecting it to be quite so bright. You know when you paint one thing you feel the urge to keep going, in this case I think I better stop right there. Here I used a spray can but it went very wrong for me I think It would of came out better if I'd used a brush and took my time, but that's just me I'm not very good with can sprays they can be very watery and run lots unless you do thin dust coats and built it up, which is what I didn't do I went in too much at once.   Here I'm trying to give you hope to try by just showing you that making something your own and giving it your own personal touch can be fun and rewarding, even with a little run of paint here and there, its fine. (Just remember to let a professional do the mechanics side ok.) I only do the cosmetics and anything I do that's anything more I always get a expert to check it, better to be safe than sorry.

I wired in a solar panel and a regulator, and again always best to double check these jobs with an expert, and this is all about not having to take out my leisure battery to charge it indoors as its very heavy. I do however think my solar panel is a little on the tiny side after fitting it, maybe that's something I will look into later down the line but for now it's charging nicely.

leisure battery, as you can see here I have used crocodile clips to attach my solar panel so I can remove it when I park it up for long periods like in winter. An easier way to get around this is to buy a camping solar panel pack, you can buy the complete unit that allows you to plug your devices into and you set up your solar panel when you park up in the best place to catch the sun. I chose to mount one in my van by the window because it was the easier option for myself, putting one on the roof would be best if you can do that, and make sure you get the proper roof seals and sealant, the last thing you need is a leaky roof. This is another reason I chose the window mount.

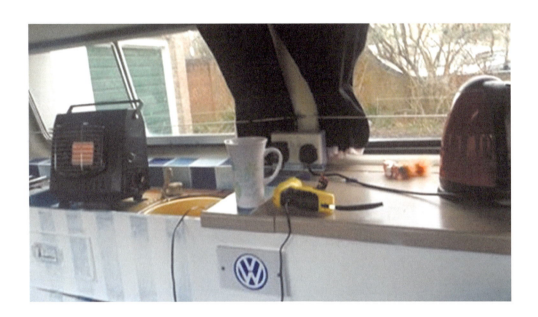

Another bad attempt at painting, four coats and I'm still not happy, still not giving up to find the right colour. Don't let this deter you it gets better. I decided at this stage me and gloss do not mix. I'm determined to keep this unit and not rip the complete thing out and start again because of all the gas pipes inside it, It would of ended up way too expensive.

Here we go it's starting to look a little brighter and I think I have found the colour and the paint I like. Sky Blue Chalk Paint and it goes on so easy but remember to seal it with varnish or wax. I have to be honest chalk paint has to be the very best paint I have ever used on furniture, if your anything like me, always have runs and imperfections, this is the paint for you. You can rub it down as well and give it that chabby - sheek look which seems all in right now.

First I put Fablon on the tables although it went on well I decided to change my mind, but it came in handy to use as a masking so I sprayed the edges of the table blue. This larger table is the perfect size for 4 to sit round comfortably but its too big to walk around once your sitting down on the bench seat. This is something I need to look into maybe making it more square shaped further down the line or mount it closer to the unit with some hooks and a folding leg. Here you will need masking tape and a can of spray, but remember to mask the entire area you don't want painted this stuff gets everywhere and make sure the masking tape is really pressed in perfectly to each edge.

So I'm in the middle of attempting to cover the under shelf area for the second time, this time in faux leather. I used a heat gun to glue it. If you have never used a heat gun the glue dries very fast on contact so best to do small areas at a time. You can also see here my solar panel mounted in the window, I used some shelf brackets I already had at home and saved money buying the brackets as well.

There was some rust around the window which I sanded back treated it with rust paint and sprayed over, I think it's starting to look a little better, each week I try and do a little something. Remember to keep the costs down by looking on free adverts for materials, you will be surprised what others no longer need that will be a treasure to you.   I will need to give this another coat or two yet. This is essential I do this now before winter comes as rust will not only look bad the damage it causes later down the line is so costly to get fixed.

As you can see here I have taken off the covers, it wasn't a easy job but worth it in the end. Tools included a screwdriver and a decent Stanley knife. With this I chose to take apart one seat piece at a time for they were all hinged up. I wrote on the under side 1.2.3.4 to and put some arrows to remember which way round they went back on, as once you cover the holes with new material its hard to see which way they go back.

I love this material, it was £25 for 5 Metre of faux leather. It's so easy to keep clean and is a lovely contrast with a soft throw over blanket.   I took each section of seat as there were four parts and covered them one at a time, pulling the material over it tightly and using a staple gun to grip to the wooden under part of each piece. To do the corners I over lapped each corner as to be tucking in a bed sheet to a mattress very neatly, this method worked and looked very tidy.

Finally starting to look brighter and cleaner, the panels on the side have also been recovered and the carpet removed. I used a staple gun to fix the material and took around 2 hours to take apart and recover. But I also did a under cover which is very important to give it a better quality finish. Here it looks slightly wrinkled because I was sitting on it to do the panel, it pushes all the air from the sponge in the seats but it does spring back up and smooth out. Obviously you can choose any material you like for any theme, I chose this because I have small children and a dog, so it's ideal to keep clean for me.

Here I've wired in a charger socket as wasn't much fun driving miles with no sat nav. Again not perfectly neat but it does the job, and the reason I mounted it here is because its close to the battery behind my seat and that is less messing about for me. While your away the last thing you need is a dead phone battery especially if you break down. I will at a later point be putting some trunking on the wires to keep them tidy.

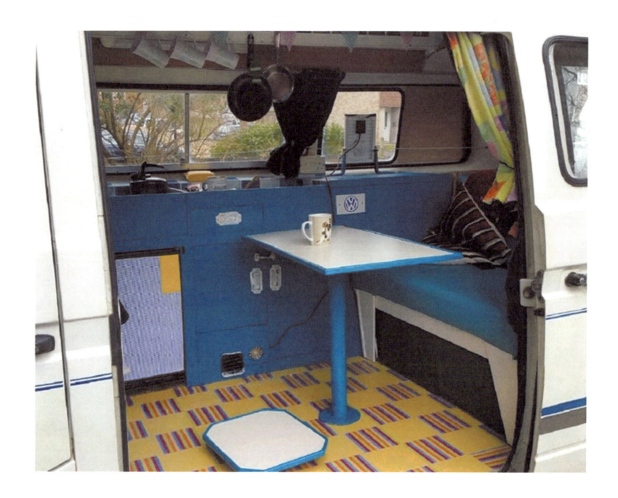

In this picture the unit has been painted in chalk paint and sealed with varnish, the floor has been put down and the tables are painted round the edges. Still a long way to go. At this point I took a few weeks break to save up a little bit as I really wanted some new curtains. I suppose in all honesty it's been more months than weeks as it all had to be done at the very lowest of cost. It's worth waiting until a bargain comes along and not to rush, in the long run you be happier to keep costs very low. If you are a VW camper owner you will understand my passion of making it personal.

Apparently it's a good idea to keep the weight of the units down in the campers so I thought what better way than to cut out some of the wood, not only that it's more attractive and softer to the eye. So here is my attempt at putting material on the doors which also was free. I pleated it with the staple gun one layer at a time.   You can see my holes are not perfectly cut but I'm getting better with practice.

This carpet on the ceiling wasn't looking very good in some patches so I cut some of it away, yet to patch this up. Perplexed for ideas at this stage but something will come along. I may end up patching it with self adhesive felt if I can find a good match in colour to the carpet already. I find this product great to work with so easy and light.

Here I'm using my photo app to decide what to do with the unit, as you can see I've drawn a line along the front trying to work out how to cut it, I wanted the sink raised up and set in the worktop but my woodworking skills as much as I say have a go, I don't know how to inset the sink because I don't have the tools, a simple jig saw isn't enough.

Ok I thought I better flash back and show you first before I covered the Bed I put this cotton under it to give it warmth and strength. This was sheets I already owned, so keeping within a low budget. Once I figured out how to take it all apart and put it back together it was a lot easier second time around when the final material arrived. The under side is made from wood so was perfect for using a staple gun to attach the materials.

I was very pleased with this buy as I happen to be passing a charity shop and seen it outside and lucky me got it for only £5. I'm yet to screw this down to the floor, but I have made a adjustment in height. I will put some extra wood in place along the front for more strength and maybe use the area under it for storage.

It's still not tidy it's a project at this stage so pottering and changing things daily. I attempted to make a mattress cover out of a red throw (right) Don't let yourself to be put off thinking there is so much to do, just take one day at a time and choose one thing that day, even if you just cover one cushion.   A lot of these vans have a small cupboard here to the right, but I like the idea of it like this as my youngest child can also lay along the width of it at the back.   I do have a child's bunk bed that sits nicely over the two front window sills as well, so we do have quite a lot of room in here.

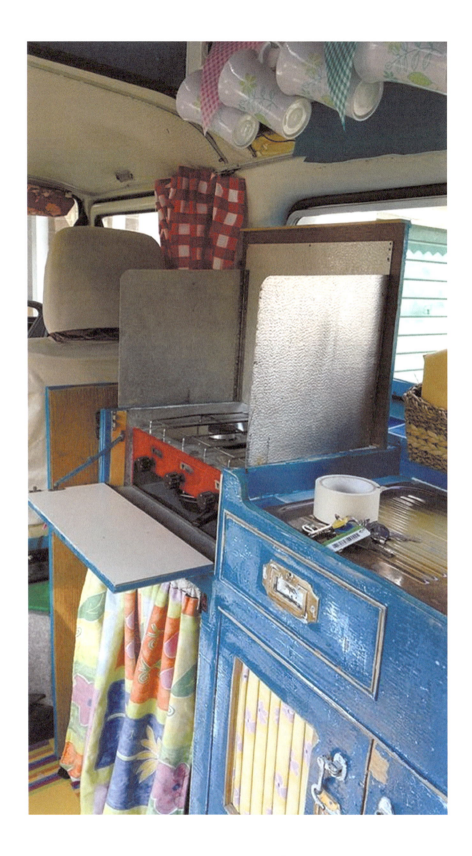

Here I've attached the cooker heat guards to the lid of the cooker, I had to make this from a shelf inside the unit as the original one had rotted. Also a curtain in the gap below where the fridge use to be as it didn't work anymore.   I may look into getting a cool box for summer. I got around this so far by buying instant coffees in them little packets with the milk already in them.

Here is the heat guard painted in a stove paint. Also I attempted to sand back the paint work to give it a rustic effect, I quite like it. But always check that the paint is specially made for cooker tops, never settle for anything less, or it could result in being very dangerous. Make sure you make it very clear what your using the paint for when you go to the store to purchase it.

Coming together nicely.... from a wider view. It's days like these that makes it all worth it. It doesn't have to be a van project you can choose one room in your house and take on a item of it each day and give it a make over, from making covers for your sofa or painting a unit or a shelf to laying a new floor. Be inspired.

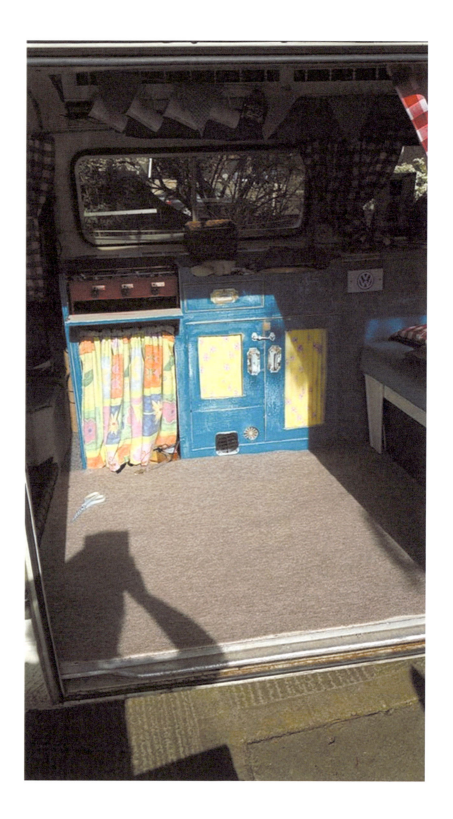

I know I already put the tile floor down, but anyone who knows me will know I can't resist a bargain. I found a roll of carpet in a charity shop for £1 and it was not only brand new, it was the perfect size and rubber backed. Now I have two options, if it gets too muddy I can roll this up and use the wipeable floor under it.

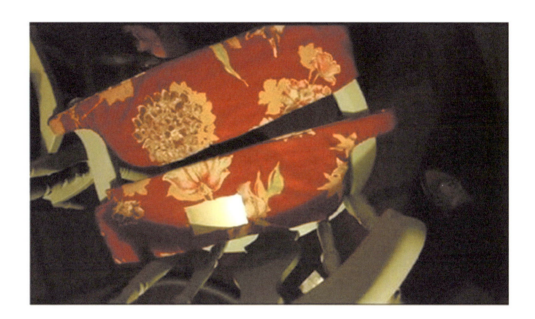

I love the fact that you can do all of these little things for free, I just used one pillow case to make these funky covers for the window sun visors. I did have to sit and hand sew them, but it was quite relaxing, and so different to all the rest. Here I just laid the visor onto 2 pieces of material pattern side face to face, drew around and sewed half a inch in which was close to the size of the visors and left a gap to insert it, after turning it right side outwards, so you end up with your pattern on the correct side.

Here you can see I've used self adhesive felt under the seat in green, I painted it first and wasn't happy with it. Who knows next week this could be entirely different again with the way things are going. Trying to get a equal feeling of soft and shiny surfaces.

This was just a bit of fun, I ran out of blankets to cut up, so painted this panel instead. Contemplating putting some Jean pockets here and using it as a craft corner for my children to put there pens in. I added some little bright bunting to it as the carpet on there felt quite rough and was very old and very dusty.

Right now I have used the Jig saw and cut out a shape in the front of the sink unit, because I couldn't raise it up, plus the wood in the way made it awkward to use the sink. I think it looks better this shape, also here I took away the tiles and added some paint to give it a rustic look.   You will be surprised what cutting a corner or cutting out a shape in a door will do for a cupboards overall look.

If you decide to take on a camper project or any project an old cupboard for example. Don't worry if your paint runs or you can't cut straight lines with a saw, just keep trying after all its only taken me five coats of paint to be happy with this one. I'm still working on the worktop waiting to find that bargain, hope one comes along soon. One of my favourite things about this camper is if I'm out and about I can stop and have a coffee any time I wish and that's such a lovely luxury, especially when you love coffee as much as me.

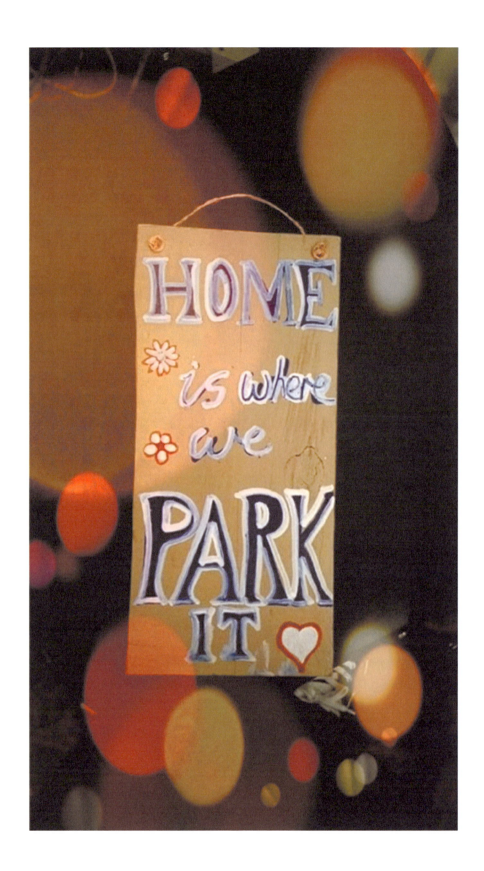

If a camper project is too big for you, how about a little sign making for fun, I made this to hang inside. How about making some for around your house, put your children's names on them maybe or your pets.

I had some old car seat covers in my garage for about two years I never thought I would even use them, so glad I kept them. They were a bit of a loose fit so I'm customising them. I did cut out the original seating cover as it was very worn, but this seat slips nicely into the shape of the frame and doesn't move as I added some ties. The back parts are still a work in progress.

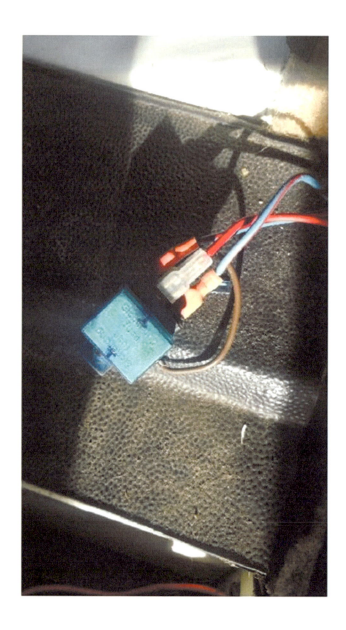

Here's a good tip. I needed to change this fuse, so take a picture before you pull out any wires so you know how to put it back correctly.

This is a better picture of the rear panel, I prefer it to the carpet its so much softer. Here you will need a screwdriver, some strong glue & scissors. Don't worry if you break some of the little clips removing the panels they don't cost very much to replace from a motor parts shop, but I used screws instead to attach mine back on.

The best thing about being nomadic is making new friends. I've watched these lads shaking hands with every jogger that's passed this morning. No seriously what a lovely view of the sea so relaxing.

Seaside

EVERY ACCOMPLISHMENT STARTS WITH THE DECISION TO TRY.

Ok the real writing on the van will not be like this thank goodness, I tried to use a photo app for ideas and I think my child could do better. But this is a great idea if you can take a photo of your project and colour it in see how it looks in different colours.

Remembering Nelly.

Today I finished wiring in a fuse to my charger socket I fitted last week, its best to be safe in case something that takes too much power is plugged into it, and fitted the hinges to my cooker lid. Because I had the VW badge missing I made this one for now, I know its funny looking but don't be afraid to be bold with your colours. My next project is to try and make a door handle up from materials I already have .. This will be some challenge but I already have a plan, this will be one unique van by time I'm finished.

Lightning Source UK Ltd.
Milton Keynes UK
UKRC02n0157050816
280015UK00008B/29